The space shuttle was
designed to launch and service
satellites in orbit.

Designer    Cooper-West
Editor    James McCarter
Art Director    Charles Matheson
Researcher    Dee Robinson
Consultant    Tony Search
Illustrators    Steve Braund
    Cooper-West

© Aladdin Books Ltd

Designed and produced by
Aladdin Books Ltd
70 Old Compton Street
London W1

First Published in the
United States in 1984 by
Franklin Watts
387 Park Avenue South
New York, NY 10016

ISBN 0-531-04817-9

Library of Congress No 84-50615

Printed in Belgium

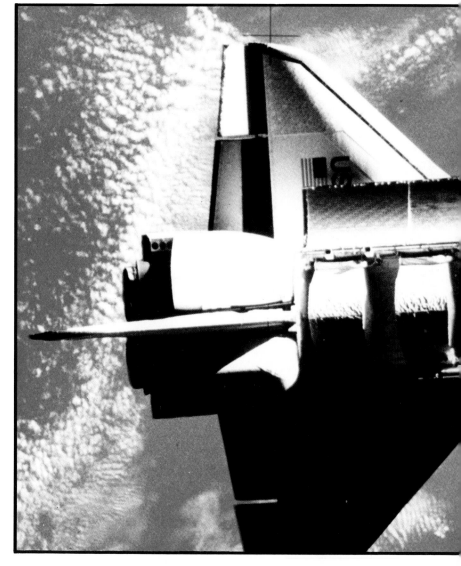

# The Electronic Revolution

# SATELLITES
## AND COMPUTERS

## Mat Irvine

**FRANKLIN WATTS**
New York·London·Toronto·Sydney

# Foreword

Satellites link up the countries of the world, relaying vast amounts of information each minute of the day. Banks and businesses use them to transfer details of day to day changes in currency exchange rates and the prices of raw materials. Every time we make an international telephone call, or watch "live" television from another continent, we use satellites.

Surveying satellites tell us more about the surface of the Earth and monitor the changing weather conditions. Navigation satellites help ships and aircraft plot their courses and have helped to save lives in emergencies. Although we are hardly aware of their presence, today's world depends upon satellite technology.

TONY SEARCH: *Technical consultant*

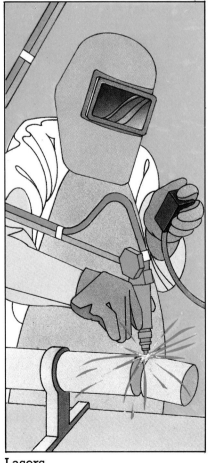

Lasers

Computers

TV and Video

# Contents

Radar and Radio

Satellites

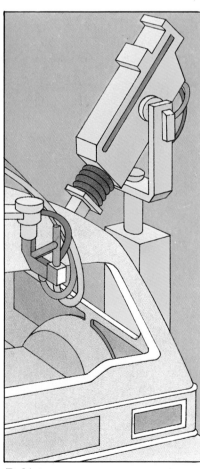

Robots

# What is a satellite?

A satellite is any object which circles, or orbits, a larger object. The first artificial satellite, Sputnik 1, was launched in 1957. Today, more than 5,000 man-made objects circle the Earth, and 300 of them are working satellites. Some can be seen at night as lights moving steadily across the sky. We use satellites to send telephone calls and television pictures, to study the land and the weather, and to navigate ships and aircraft.

## Satellites and electronics

Satellites rely on electronic circuits to make them work. These receive and transmit signals and control the satellite in orbit. As circuits are made increasingly smaller, more can be built into the limited space on board, and the satellite can do more complicated work. A single communications satellite can now carry up to 12,000 telephone calls at one time.

▽ The word "satellite" does not apply only to man-made objects. The Moon is the natural satellite of the Earth, while the Earth and the other planets are satellites of the Sun.

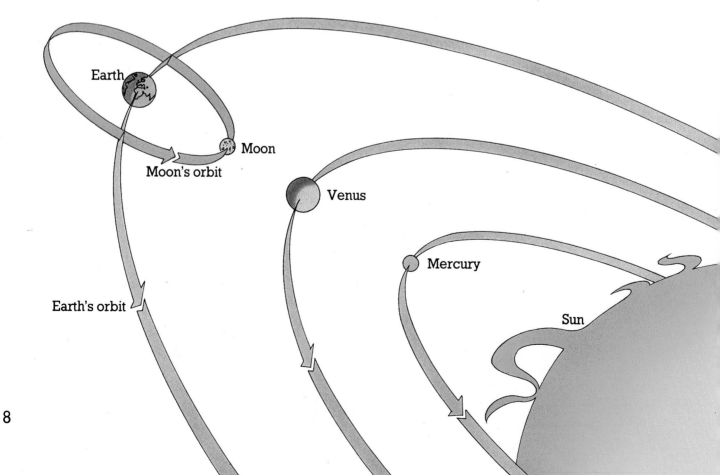

Earth

Moon

Moon's orbit

Venus

Mercury

Earth's orbit

Sun

△ In the comfort of your own home, you can see on TV what the weather will be like. The pictures come from satellites that are orbiting the Earth many thousands of kilometers above our heads.

▷ Sputnik 1 was very simple compared with modern satellites. It was just 64 cm (25 ins) in diameter and it sent out only a "bleep bleep" radio signal. Sputnik 1 spent three months in orbit.

# Getting into orbit

Many satellites are put into orbit by rockets, which are used only once and then jettisoned in space. Today, satellites are also launched from the space shuttle, a reusable spacecraft, designed for a life of up to 100 missions.

## Rockets

A rocket engine works by burning fuel to produce a stream of hot gases. The gases push against the rocket, propelling it forward. Early rockets, used as weapons, were powered by solid fuel, like giant fireworks. Solid fuels are simple to make and can be stored for a long time. In the 1920s, however, the first rocket propelled by liquid fuel was launched. This method proved more powerful. Most modern rockets use liquid fuel, though some, like the space shuttle, use both types.

2nd Stage

1st Stage

△ To launch satellites, rockets use a method called "staging." This European Space Agency Ariane rocket is putting a Meteosat weather satellite into space. One rocket stage alone could not carry enough fuel to put the satellite into orbit, so a second and third stage are used as well. When each stage has burned up all its fuel, it drops away and the next one fires.

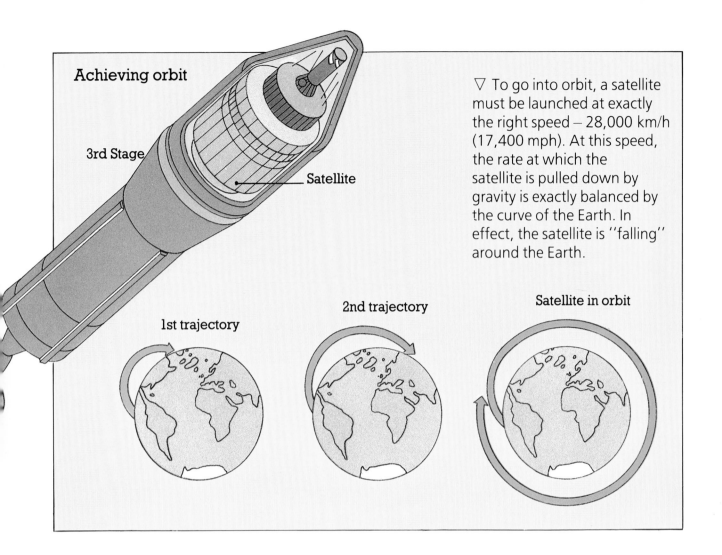

## Achieving orbit

3rd Stage

Satellite

▽ To go into orbit, a satellite must be launched at exactly the right speed – 28,000 km/h (17,400 mph). At this speed, the rate at which the satellite is pulled down by gravity is exactly balanced by the curve of the Earth. In effect, the satellite is "falling" around the Earth.

1st trajectory

2nd trajectory

Satellite in orbit

▷ The space shuttle can launch satellites from its payload bay. Future missions should make it possible to repair satellites that have gone wrong in orbit. Because most of the shuttle is reusable, launching satellites should eventually become much less expensive.

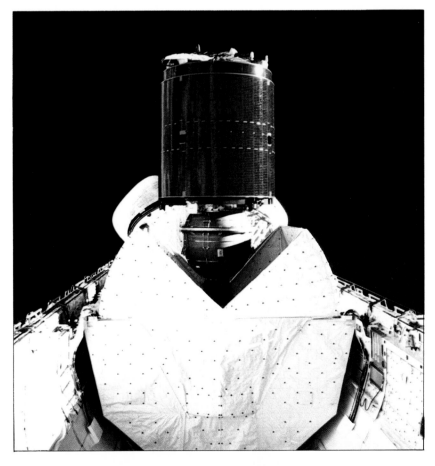

# Different orbits

Satellites are placed in different orbits around the Earth according to the job they are designed to do. For example, a satellite that surveys the Earth's lands and oceans is placed in a polar orbit, orbiting above the North and the South Poles. As the satellite orbits, the Earth rotates under its path, so that every part of the Earth eventually passes beneath it. After a certain number of days, the satellite will pass above the same area as before and photograph it again. The two pictures can then be compared for any changes that may have occurred.

## Communications satellites

Communications satellites – or Comsats – occupy a geostationary orbit far above the Equator. Here they orbit at exactly the same speed as the Earth rotates, and in the same direction, so they appear to be stationary over one point on the Equator. Because they are in a fixed position, Comsats are used to relay inter-continental telephone calls and "live" television programs.

▷ Communications satellites allow programs to be broadcast directly into remote areas. Here a dish aerial on the left is picking up the signals from the satellite. The picture can be shown on an ordinary television set. This system is most useful for transmitting educational programs.

▽ Two types of orbit. The polar orbit satellite travels at a height of about 1,000 km (620 miles) and is constantly passing over a different part of the Earth. The satellite in geostationary orbit travels at a height of 36,000 km (22,300 miles) and always appears to be in the same position over the Equator.

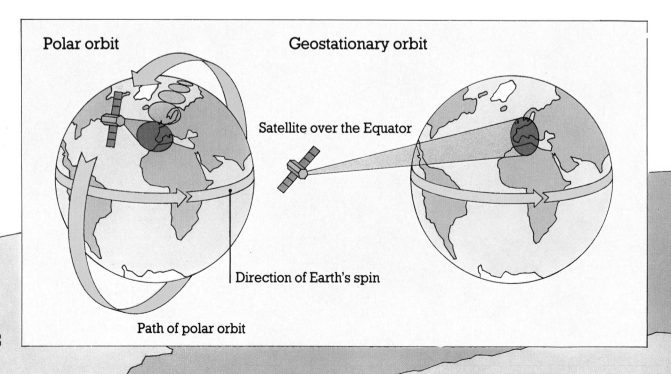

Polar orbit

Geostationary orbit

Satellite over the Equator

Direction of Earth's spin

Path of polar orbit

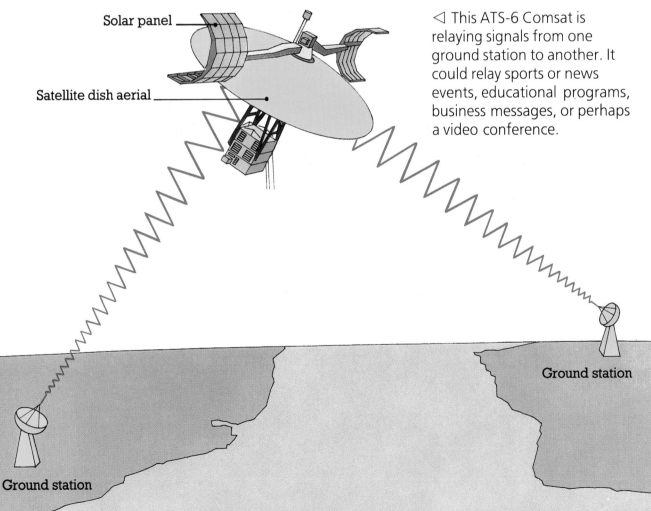

Solar panel

Satellite dish aerial

◁ This ATS-6 Comsat is relaying signals from one ground station to another. It could relay sports or news events, educational programs, business messages, or perhaps a video conference.

Ground station

Ground station

# Weather satellites

One of the most important uses of satellites is in weather forecasting. Every day, weather satellites look down on the Earth, photographing the constantly changing cloud patterns. Pictures from the satellites are transmitted by radio to ground stations. There, computers "enhance" the pictures, electronically processing the radio signals to bring out greater details. Satellite information has led to a greater understanding of the world's weather systems and to more accurate forecasts.

## Satellite warnings

Some weather satellites are placed in a geostationary orbit. Because they are always above the same part of the Earth, they observe changes in the weather as soon as they occur. More dramatically, they can track the course of hurricanes and tornadoes, and give people living in their paths adequate early warning.

▽ Five weather satellites — one European, one Japanese and three American — are in geostationary orbit. Among them they cover every part of the Earth, so that weathermen can build up a complete picture of the Earth's weather at any one time.

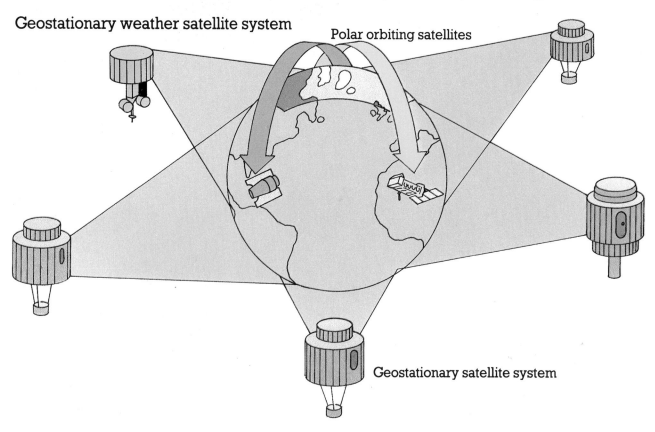

Geostationary weather satellite system

Polar orbiting satellites

Geostationary satellite system

▷ A computer-enhanced picture of Hurricane Alicia. The colors show up different temperatures in the storm. This can help the weathermen to predict how quickly the storm will develop and in what direction it will probably travel.

▽ A hurricane begins to form far out in the ocean. Modern weather satellites can spot this danger and warn people on land long before the hurricane arrives.

# Satellites and navigation

Even the largest ships are tiny compared with the sea. But navigation satellites now enable a captain with the right equipment to determine exactly where his ship is at any time, day or night. Navigation satellites circle the Earth above the Equator in a geostationary orbit, giving out radio signals that are picked up by a tracking dish aerial on board the ship. A computer uses these signals to calculate the ship's position to within a few hundred meters.

▷ A ship's navigation officer looks at information supplied over a teleprinter link. This information, received via satellite, may give him up-to-the-minute details of weather and other conditions.

## One satellite with many uses

Navigation satellites are also used for communications. They provide ship-to-shore telephone links, and relay radio broadcasts and information from weather stations. In an emergency, the satellite relays an automatic distress signal from the ship to alert the rescue services.

▽ A ship is in trouble at sea, and an aircraft has crashed in the mountains. But each contains a small emergency transmitter which can send a signal via satellite to ground stations. Using signals from three or more satellites, rescuers can accurately locate the position of the crash.

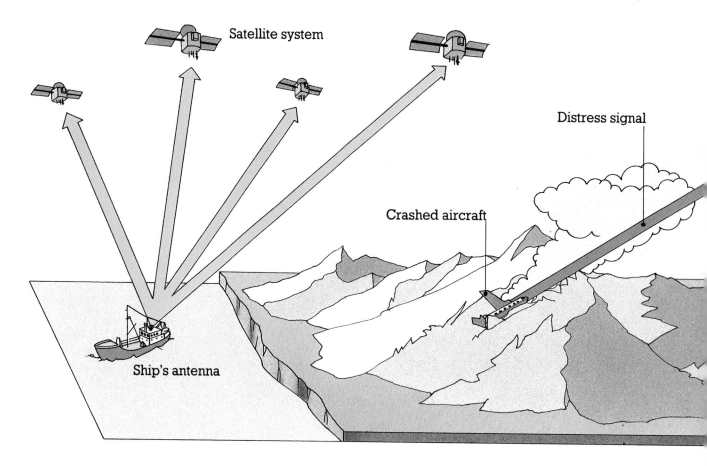

Satellite system

Distress signal

Crashed aircraft

Ship's antenna

## The Navstar navigation satellite system

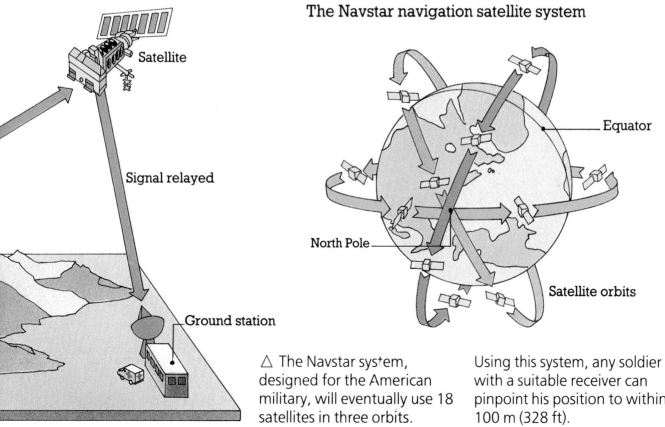

Satellite

Signal relayed

Ground station

Equator

North Pole

Satellite orbits

△ The Navstar system, designed for the American military, will eventually use 18 satellites in three orbits.

Using this system, any soldier with a suitable receiver can pinpoint his position to within 100 m (328 ft).

# Earthwatch

Satellites give us a unique "bird's eye" view of our planet. From a height of many hundreds of kilometers, the Earth's surface can be seen in great detail. Some of the rock patterns observed in this way have indicated where valuable minerals may be found. Earth resources satellites, such as the Landsat series, have been designed to spot such features.

## Mapping land and sea

The photographs taken by Landsat have been used to make very accurate maps. In addition, pictures taken with infra-red cameras, and then enhanced by computer, can show up diseases in crops long before they are noticed on the ground. Over the oceans, similar Seasat satellites are used to measure the temperatures of different ocean currents.

▽ Landsat 4, the fourth and last satellite in the Landsat series, carries two main instruments: a camera and a thermic mapper, which builds up pictures from heat patterns. Solar panels generate electricity to power the craft, and the antenna sends signals back to Earth.

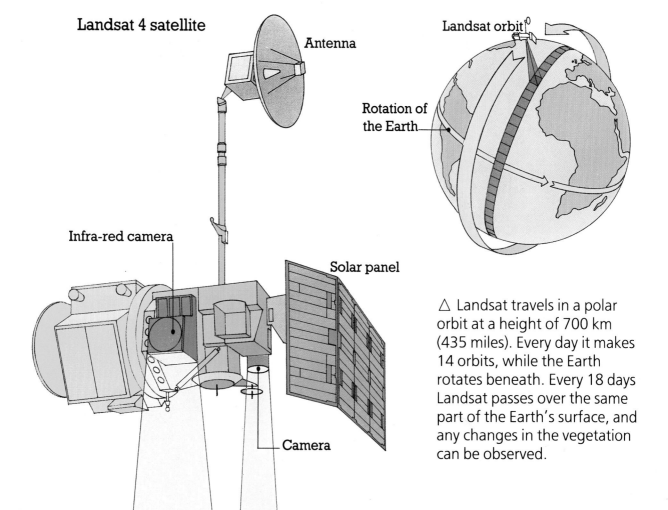

**Landsat 4 satellite**

Antenna

Infra-red camera

Solar panel

Camera

Landsat orbit

Rotation of the Earth

△ Landsat travels in a polar orbit at a height of 700 km (435 miles). Every day it makes 14 orbits, while the Earth rotates beneath. Every 18 days Landsat passes over the same part of the Earth's surface, and any changes in the vegetation can be observed.

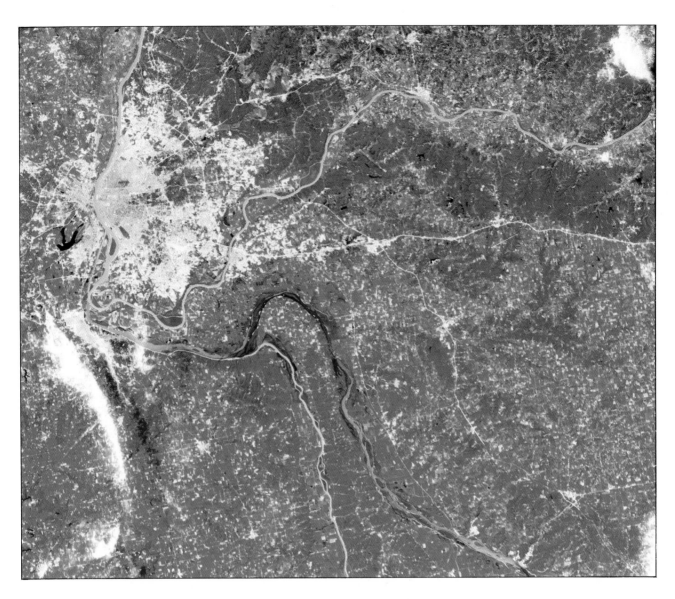

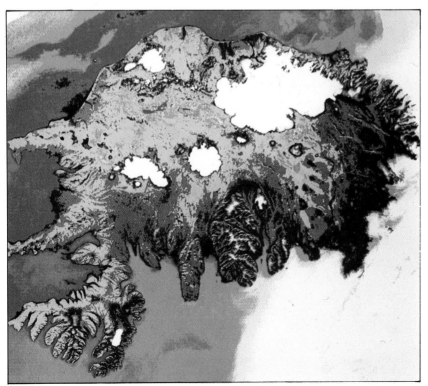

△ An infra-red picture of the St. Louis area taken by Landsat. This shows up details that otherwise would not be obvious. Cultivated fields show up as a different pattern from the forests. An experienced person will be able to tell different crops and trees from one another.

◁ Iceland pictured by a thermal mapper instrument. The different colors show up the different temperatures of the island. The tops of the mountains are white. The hottest part of Iceland, the geothermal springs, appear as red.

19

# Space probes

Space probes differ from satellites in that they are not placed in orbit, but are sent away from Earth to explore other parts of the solar system. The first probes were launched to explore the Moon. Others followed that were sent to the Sun and the nearby planets of Mars and Venus. The Mariner probes actually landed on Mars and analyzed samples of the Martian soil.

## Automatic control

Two Voyager probes were sent to Jupiter, Saturn and the other outer planets of the solar system. Because radio signals had to travel huge distances to reach the probes, the Voyagers were programmed to work automatically. On-board computers kept the probes on course and directed their cameras to take unique photographs of the planets and their moons.

▽ Voyager took this picture of the planet Jupiter from a height of many thousands of kilometers. The largest object is the Great Red Spot, thought to be a gigantic storm system floating in the atmosphere. Its size is greater than the diameter of the Earth.

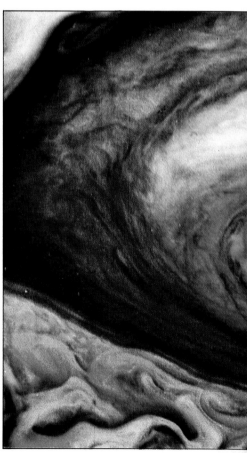

△ The surface of Mars, as photographed by Viking 2. The red color of the planet shows up very well, and the sky is tinted pink. The Viking probes sent back many pictures of Mars, both from the surface and from orbit.

◁ Before any probe can be launched, careful checks must be made. Once in space it cannot be repaired.
Here, engineers check that Viking 2 has no dust particles inside which could float about and cause damage.

# Manned satellites

The first manned spaceflight was made in 1961, by Yuri Gagarin of the Soviet Union. Since then, spaceflights have been of longer and longer duration. The current record for staying in space is over six months, set by a Soviet cosmonaut on board the Salyut space station. These extended missions have shown that being in space has no ill-effects on people, as had once been feared.

## Working in space

On board a spacecraft or space station in orbit, the effects of Earth's gravity are not felt. This allows scientists to perform experiments that would be extremely expensive or even impossible to carry out on Earth. Experiments conducted on board Salyut, and on the European Spacelab carried into orbit by the space shuttle, have shown that certain complex drugs and microelectronic circuits could be manufactured more cheaply and easily in space.

▷ Astronauts inside the European Spacelab during its first flight. In the free fall conditions they can move freely around and use all the surfaces of the orbiting laboratory.

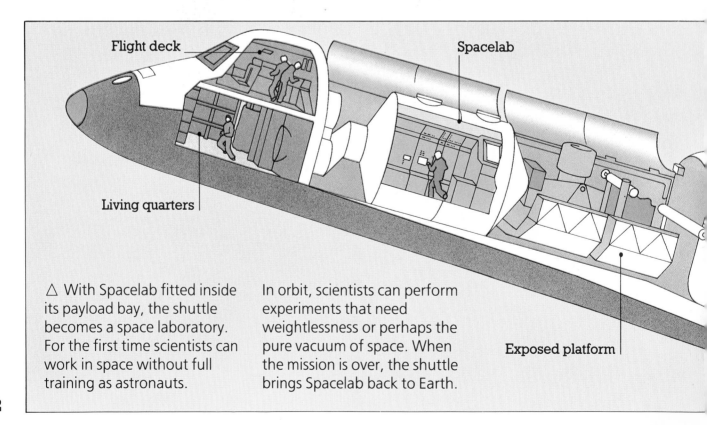

Flight deck

Spacelab

Living quarters

Exposed platform

△ With Spacelab fitted inside its payload bay, the shuttle becomes a space laboratory. For the first time scientists can work in space without full training as astronauts.

In orbit, scientists can perform experiments that need weightlessness or perhaps the pure vacuum of space. When the mission is over, the shuttle brings Spacelab back to Earth.

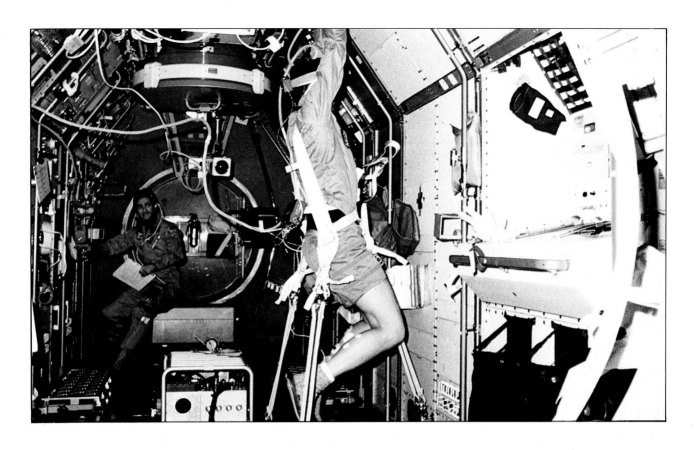

▷ Soviet space stations, called Salyut, have been launched for many years. The latest, Salyut 7, is visited by cosmonauts traveling in the Soyuz craft. Supplies are brought up by the unmanned Progress craft.

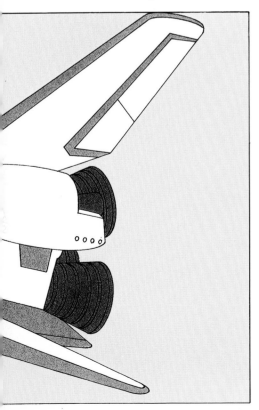

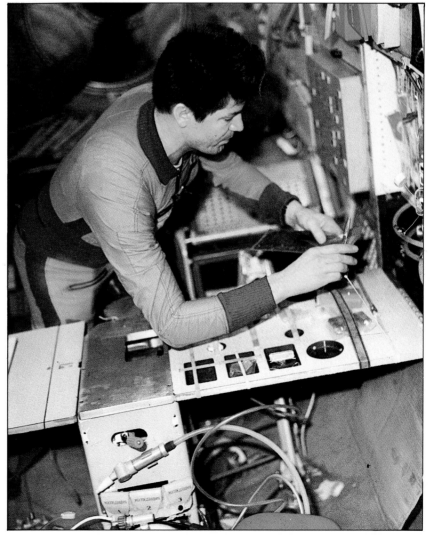

# Military satellites

Satellites have been used for military purposes since they were first launched. Military communications satellites link armed forces all over the world with their headquarters. Navigational satellites, such as Navstar, allow military personnel to pinpoint exactly where they are, using their portable radio receivers.

## The view from space

Spy satellites, such as the American "Big Bird," are used to observe strategic installations, taking photographs showing for example, the number of tanks in a battalion, enemy missile sites, or the aircraft on an airfield. Scientists are now experimenting with satellite-mounted laser-beam weapons. These will be able to stay in orbit and knock out enemy missiles and satellites in space.

▷ The photographs from spy satellites, such as Big Bird (inset), are thought to be as much as 100 times more detailed than those taken by surveying satellites. Some spy satellites drop as low as 100 km (62 miles) to take their pictures, then boost back into a higher orbit.

▽ Film taken by a spy satellite is placed in a capsule, which re-enters the Earth's atmosphere and floats down by parachute. An aircraft snatches the capsule out of the air. If the information was transmitted by radio, like Landsat's, it could be intercepted by the enemy.

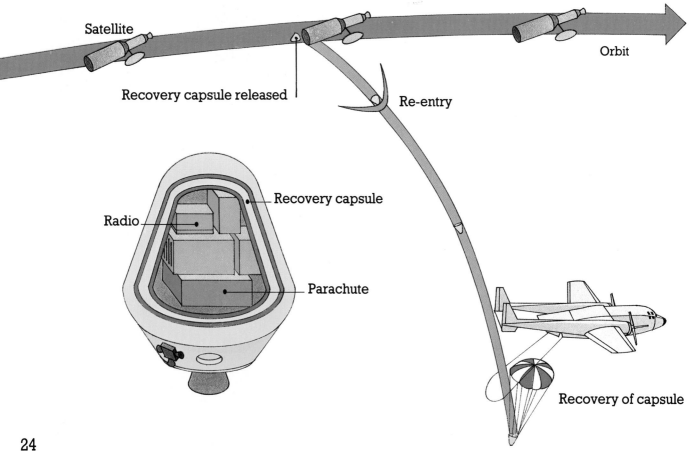

Satellite

Orbit

Recovery capsule released

Re-entry

Recovery capsule

Radio

Parachute

Recovery of capsule

# The future in space

The American space agency, NASA, plans to build a permanent space station by 1994, using materials transported by the shuttle. Scientists and engineers on board would continue the work begun in Salyut and Spacelab, making products and performing experiments in weightless conditions. Free of the Earth's atmosphere, which blocks out some starlight, telescopes would be used in space to look deeper into the universe. Giant solar panels would collect energy from the Sun to power the space stations or perhaps to beam it down for use on Earth.

▽ Giant power satellites could be built using materials transported by the shuttle. They would collect energy from the Sun, convert it to microwaves and beam it down to give us power on Earth.

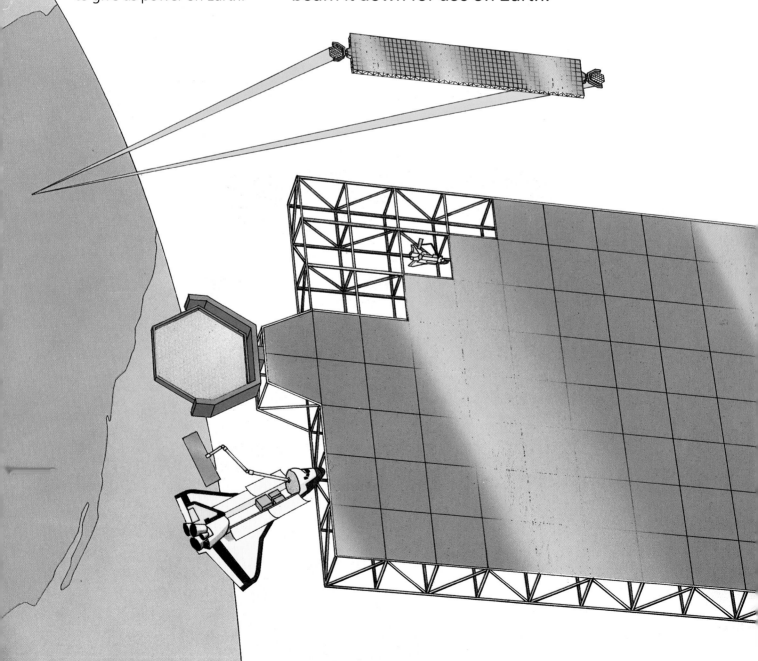

## Travel to the planets

With permanent space stations established, travel to the Moon and planets would become much easier. Spaceships could be built in Earth orbit, fuelled and sent on their way carrying the explorers of the future.

## Mining the asteroids

Looking further ahead, it may be possible to tow asteroids into Earth orbit. There they could be mined for minerals they contained. These minerals might be used to build a huge space station where thousands of people could live and work. Such ideas sound fantastic, but space technology has come a long way in the short time since the first satellite was launched.

▽ Asteroids could be towed into Earth orbit and mined to provide raw materials for space factories. Some of the materials might be used to build a space colony like that shown in the picture.

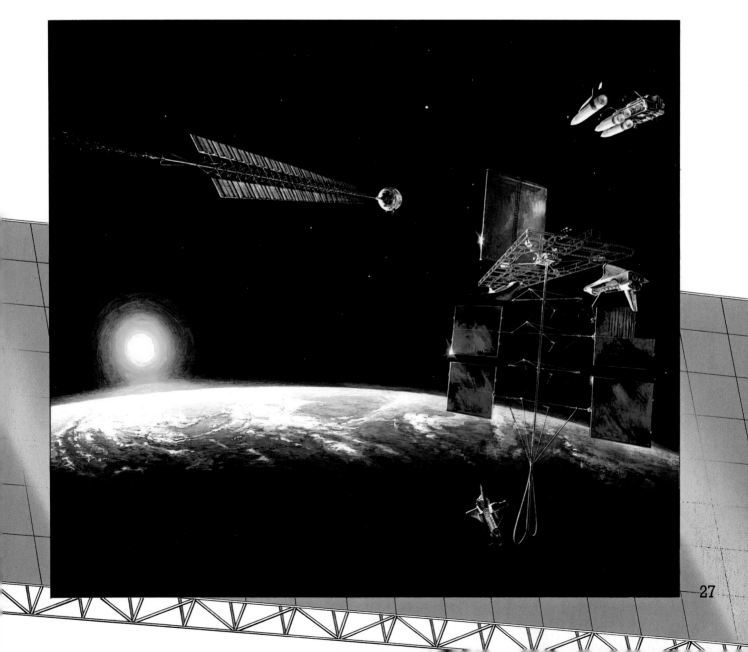

# Glossary

**Communications Satellite**  A satellite that can relay television, telephone and similar signals from one point on Earth to another. A shortened name is Comsat, and most are in geostationary orbit.

**Free Fall**  Satellites in orbit do not feel the force of gravity as we do on Earth. They are said to be in free fall or weightless conditions.

**Geostationary Orbit**  The orbit above the Earth's equator, 36,000 km (22,300 miles) high, where a satellite travels at exactly the same speed as the Earth rotates and about the same axis, so it appears stationary. Also known as a Synchronous or Clarke Orbit (the last after Arthur C. Clarke, who described this type of orbit in 1945).

**Global Positioning Satellite**  Satellites that pin-point a position on the Earth to within 100 m (328 ft). Usually four such satellites give an accurate "fix".

**Satellite**  An object in orbit around another – called the parent body. A man-made object is called an artificial satellite. A moon around a planet is a natural satellite.

**Solar Panel**  A set of photoelectric cells that generate electricity from sunlight. Used by many satellites.

**Space Factory**  A large space station used to manufacture items that would be expensive or impossible to make on Earth.

**Space Probe**  A "satellite" that travels away from the Earth. It may travel to the Moon, Sun or planets.

**Spy Satellite**  A satellite that can photograph "behind enemy lines." Usually the pictures are returned to Earth as photographic film in a capsule.

# Index

## Acknowledgements
*The publishers wish to thank the following people who have helped in the preparation of this book:*
Centre National D'Etudes Spatiales, European Space Agency, Inmarsat, Marconi, Military Archives and Research Services, NASA, Novosti, Rose Lockwood, Tass, UK National Remote Sensing Centre.

## Photographic Credits:
*Cover*: Centre National D'etudes spatiales, *title page*: NASA, page 9: EEA/Mat Irvine, page 11: NASA (Space Frontiers), page 13: NASA, page 15: NASA (Space Frontiers), page 17: Racal Decca, page 19: Tony Stone; Space Frontiers, page 20: Space Frontiers, page 21: NASA, page 23: Space Frontiers; Tass News Agency, page 25: Mat Irvine; Aerofilms, page 27: Mat Irvine.